Pre-Writing Skills Exercises

Writing Book for Toddlers
Children's Reading & Writing Books

Practice makes perfect! Complete these fun exercises and improve your handwriting at the same time!

Trace the lines from left to right.

Trace the lines from right to left.

TRACING LINES

Trace the lines from top to bottom.

TRACING LINES

Trace the lines from bottom to top.

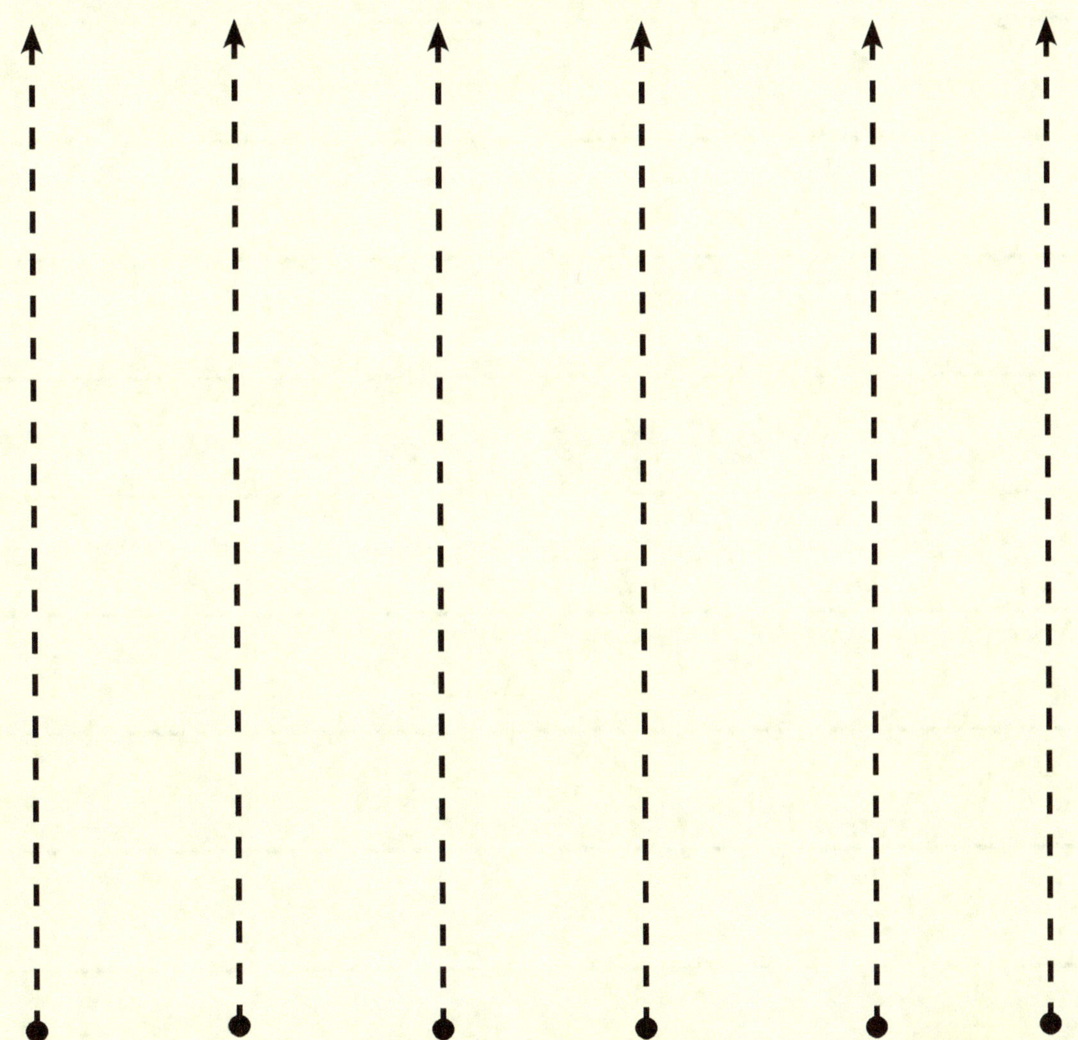

TRACING LINES

Trace the lines in each row.

TRACING LINES

Trace the lines in each row.

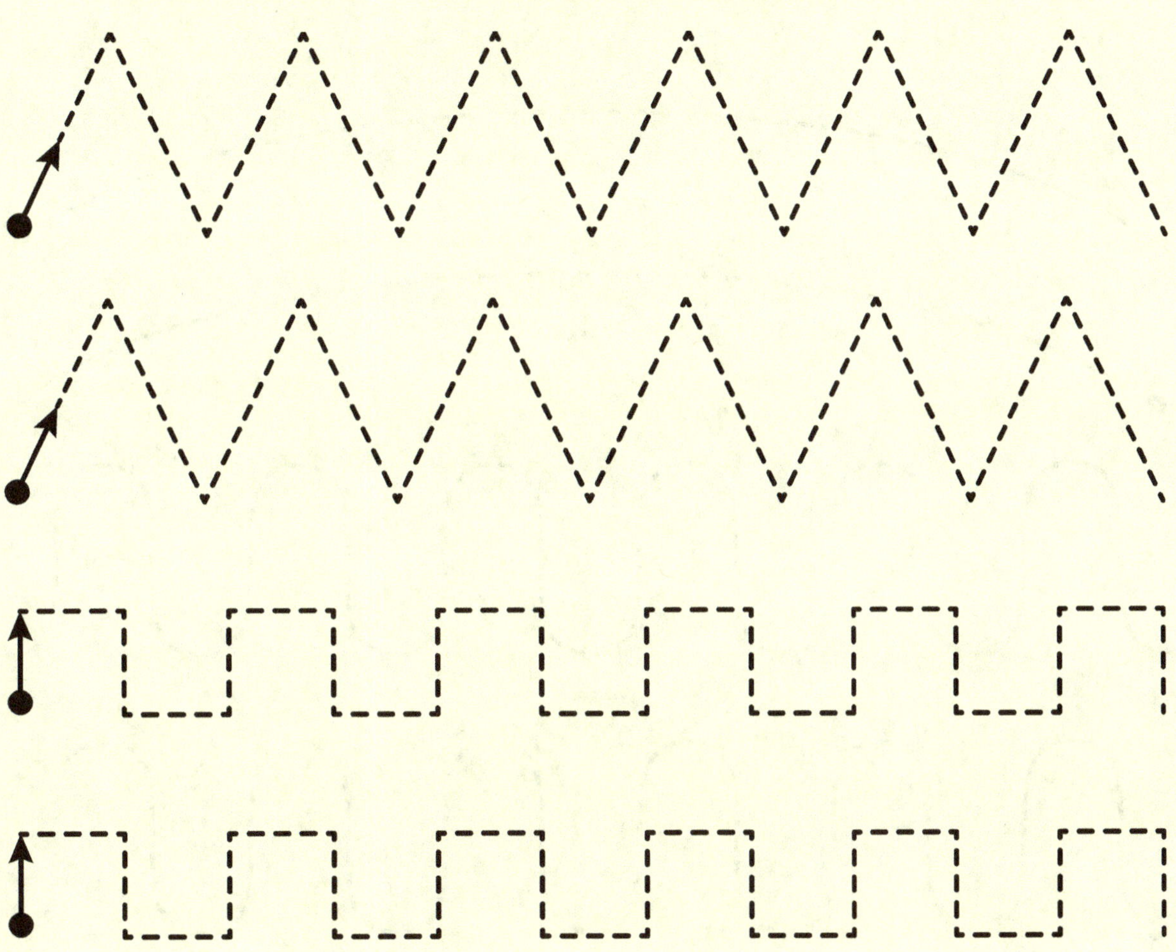

TRACING LINES

Trace the lines in each row.

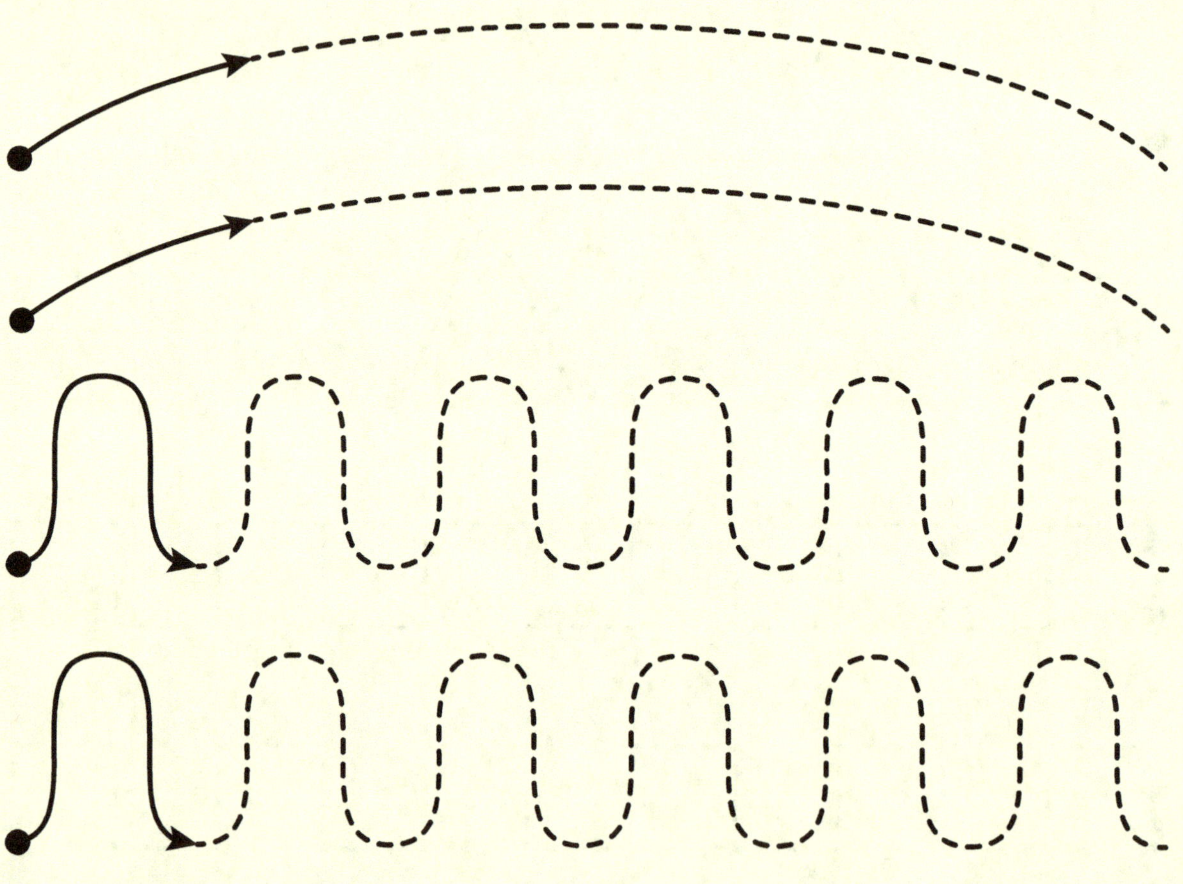

TRACING LINES

Trace the lines in each row.

TRACING LINES

Trace the lines in each row.

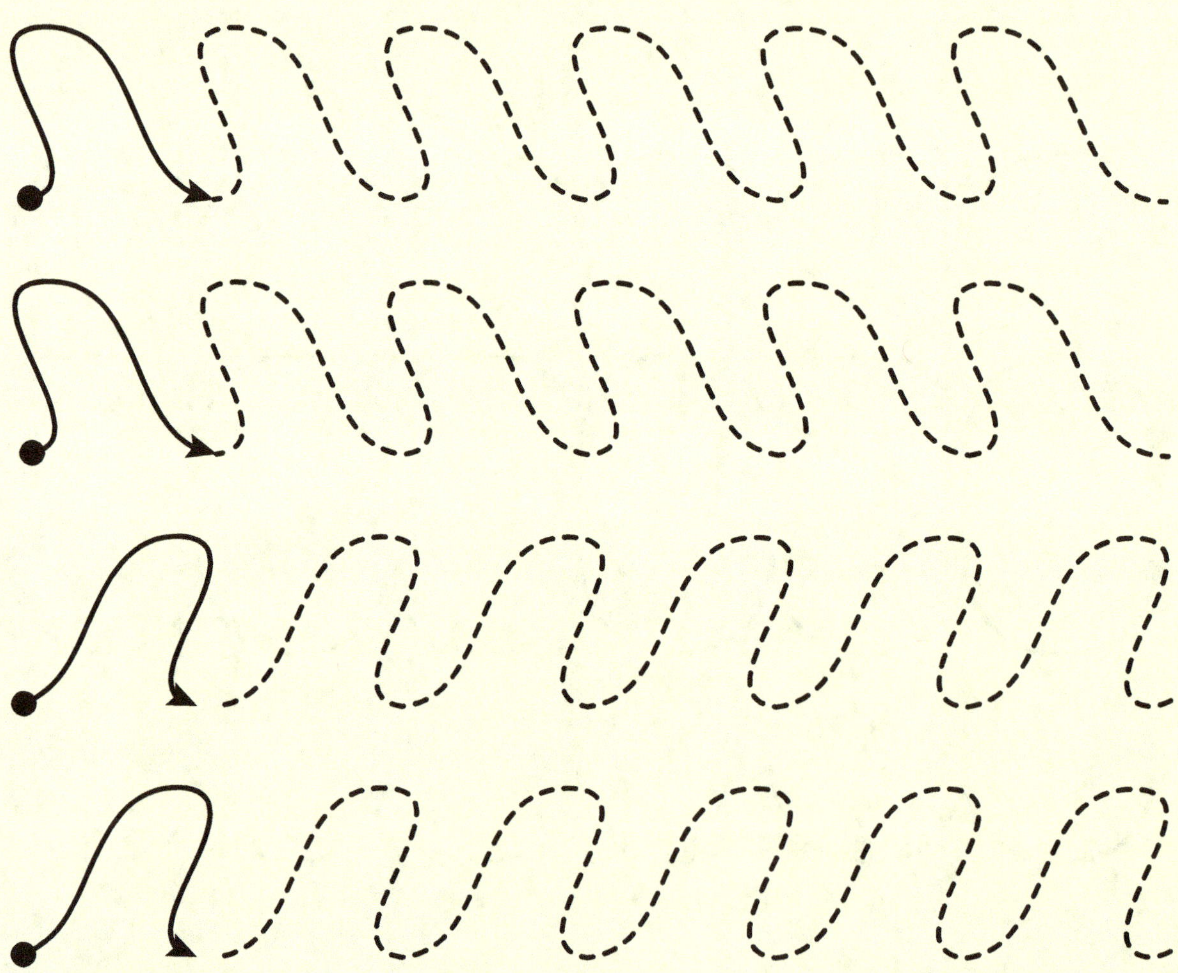

TRACING LINES

Trace the lines in each row.

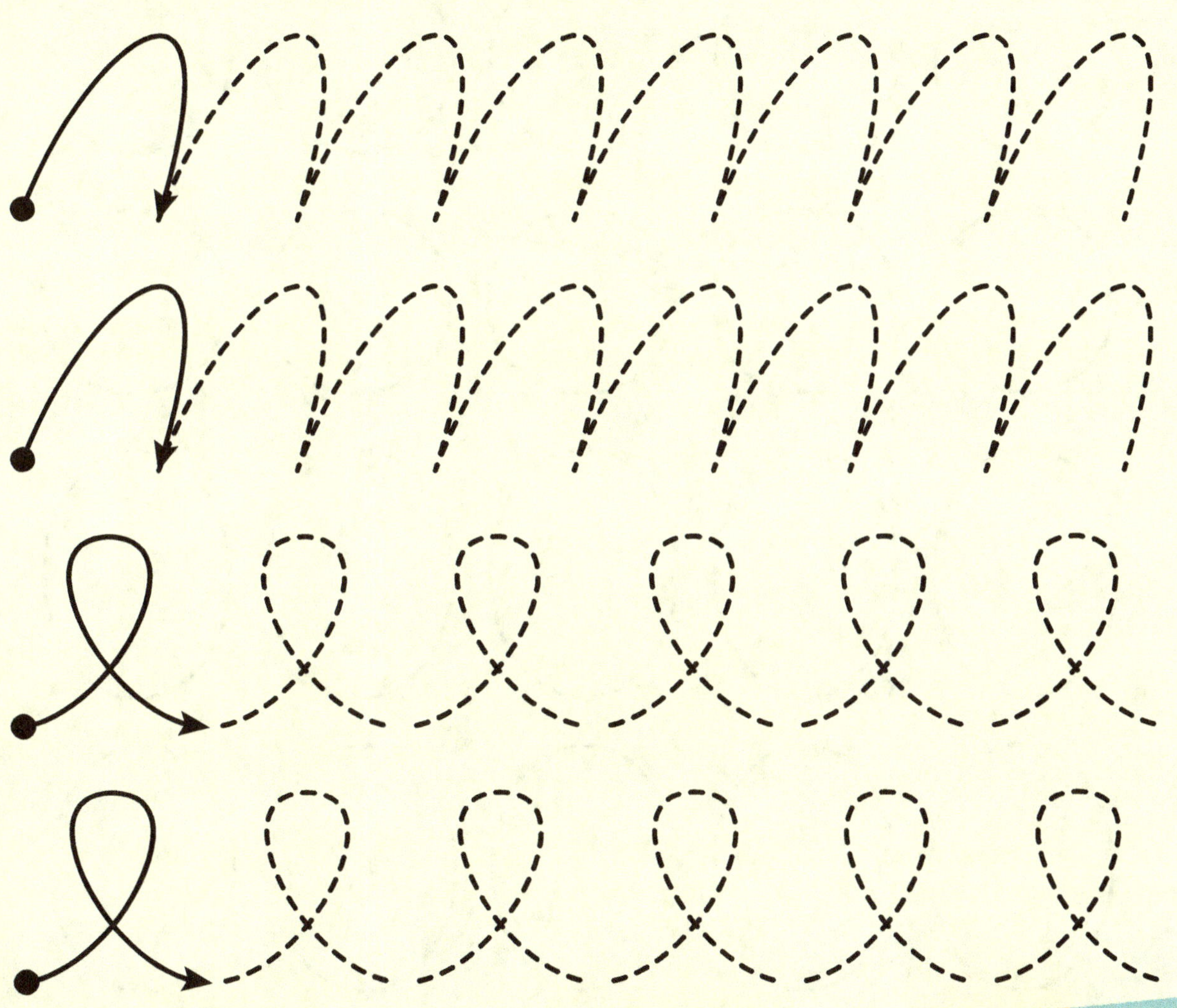

TRACING SHAPES

Trace the lines in each row.

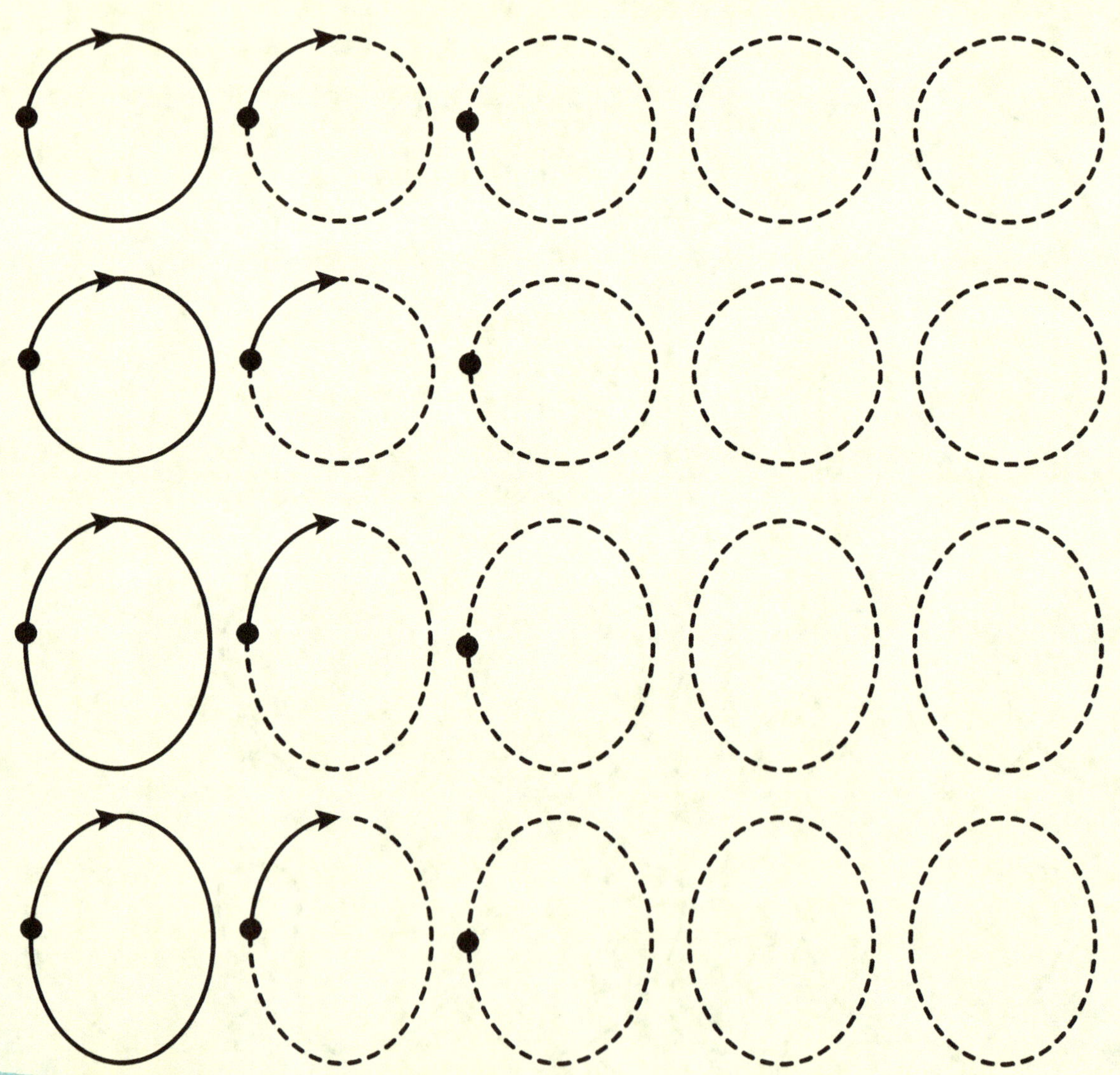

TRACING SHAPES

Trace the lines in each row.

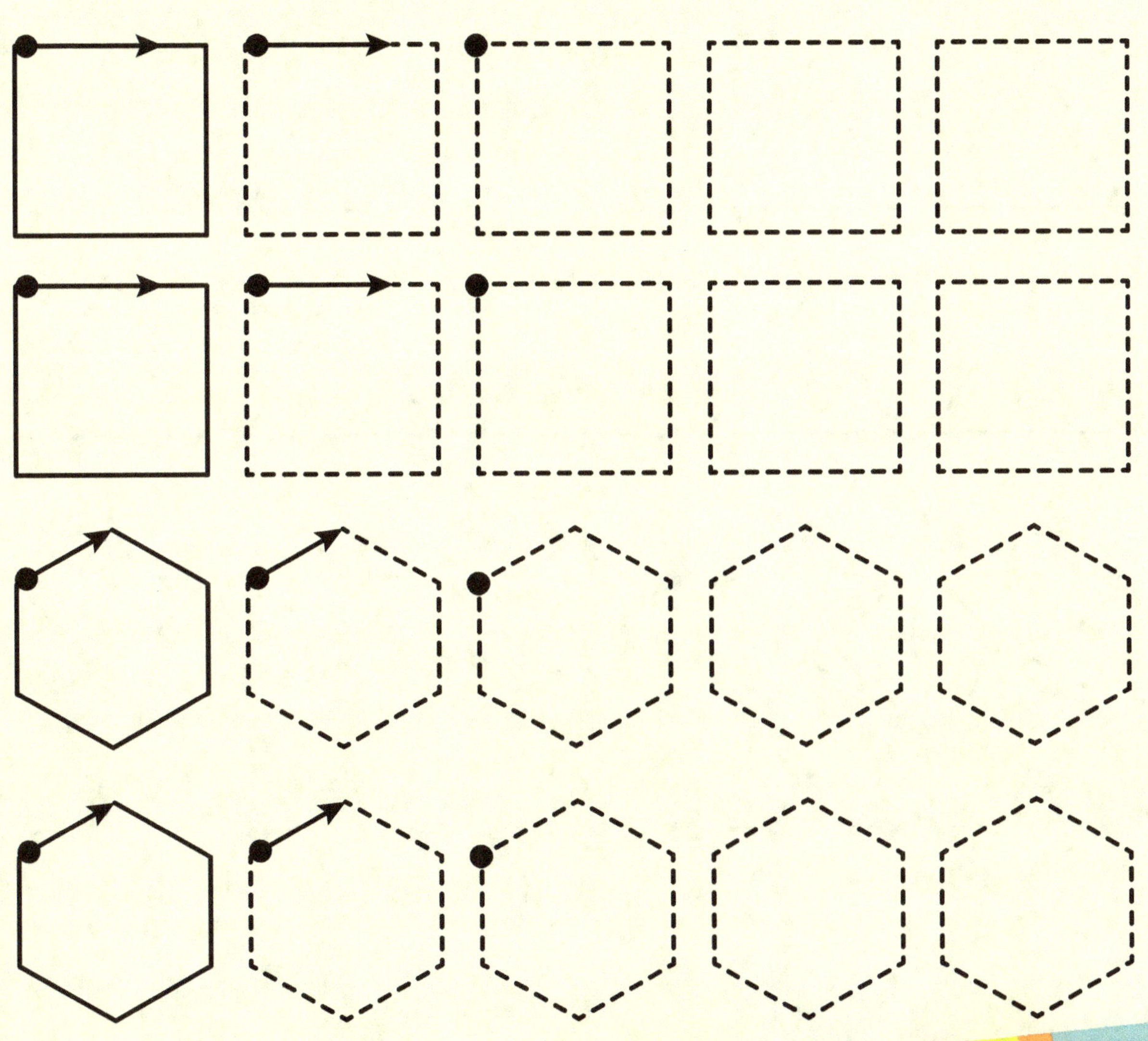

Trace the lines in each row.

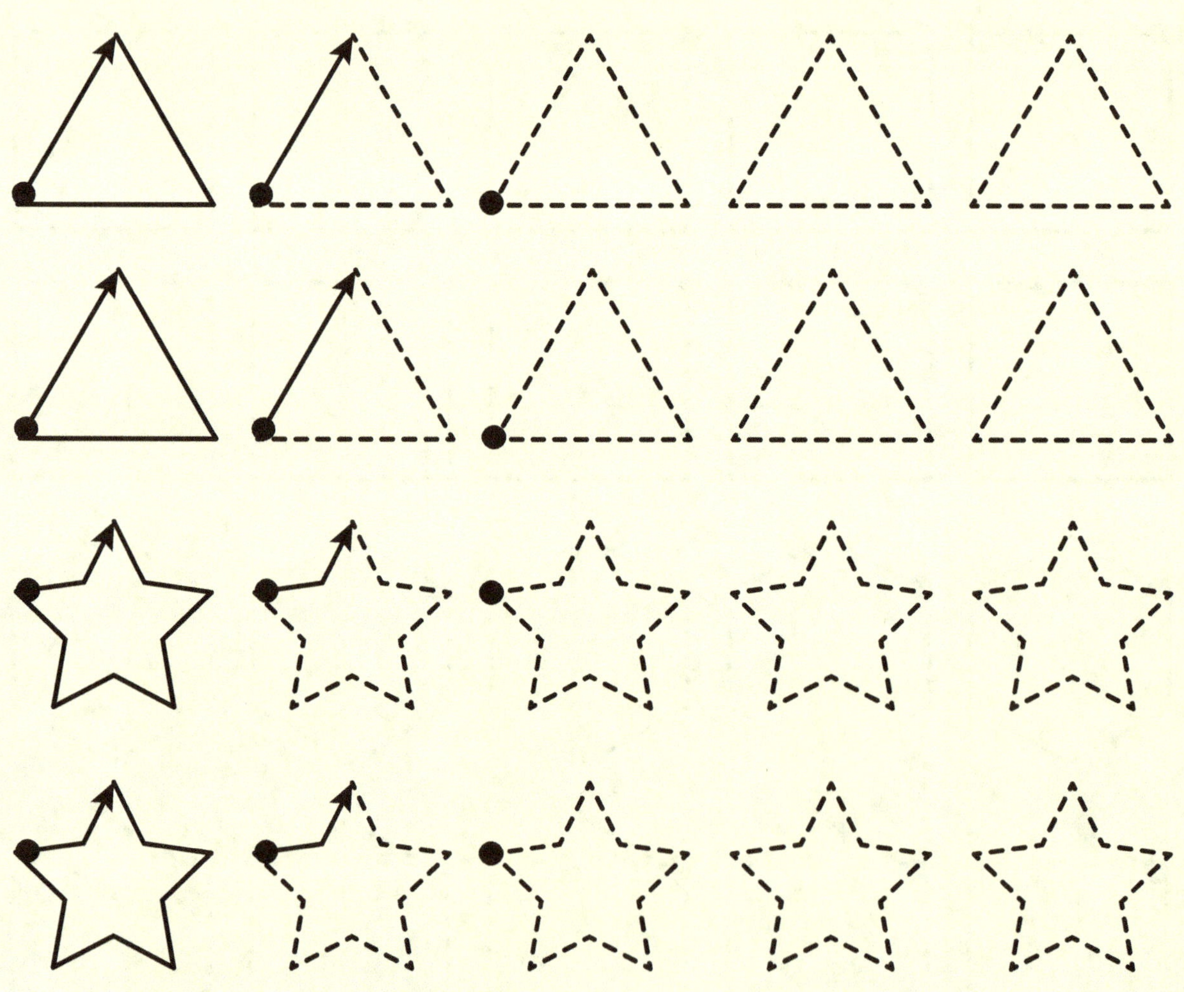

TRACING SHAPES

Trace the lines in each row.

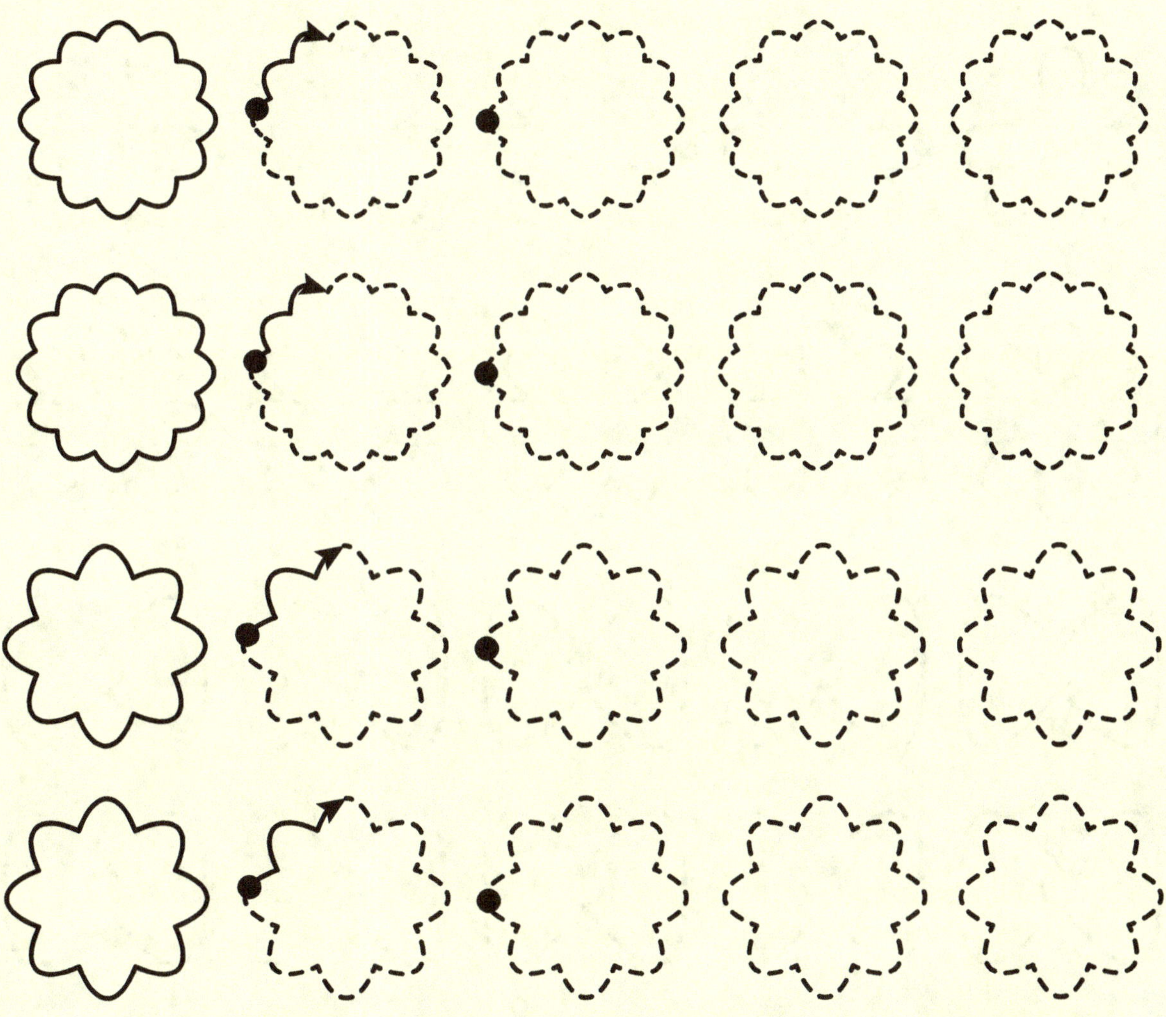

TRACING SHAPES

Trace the lines in each row.

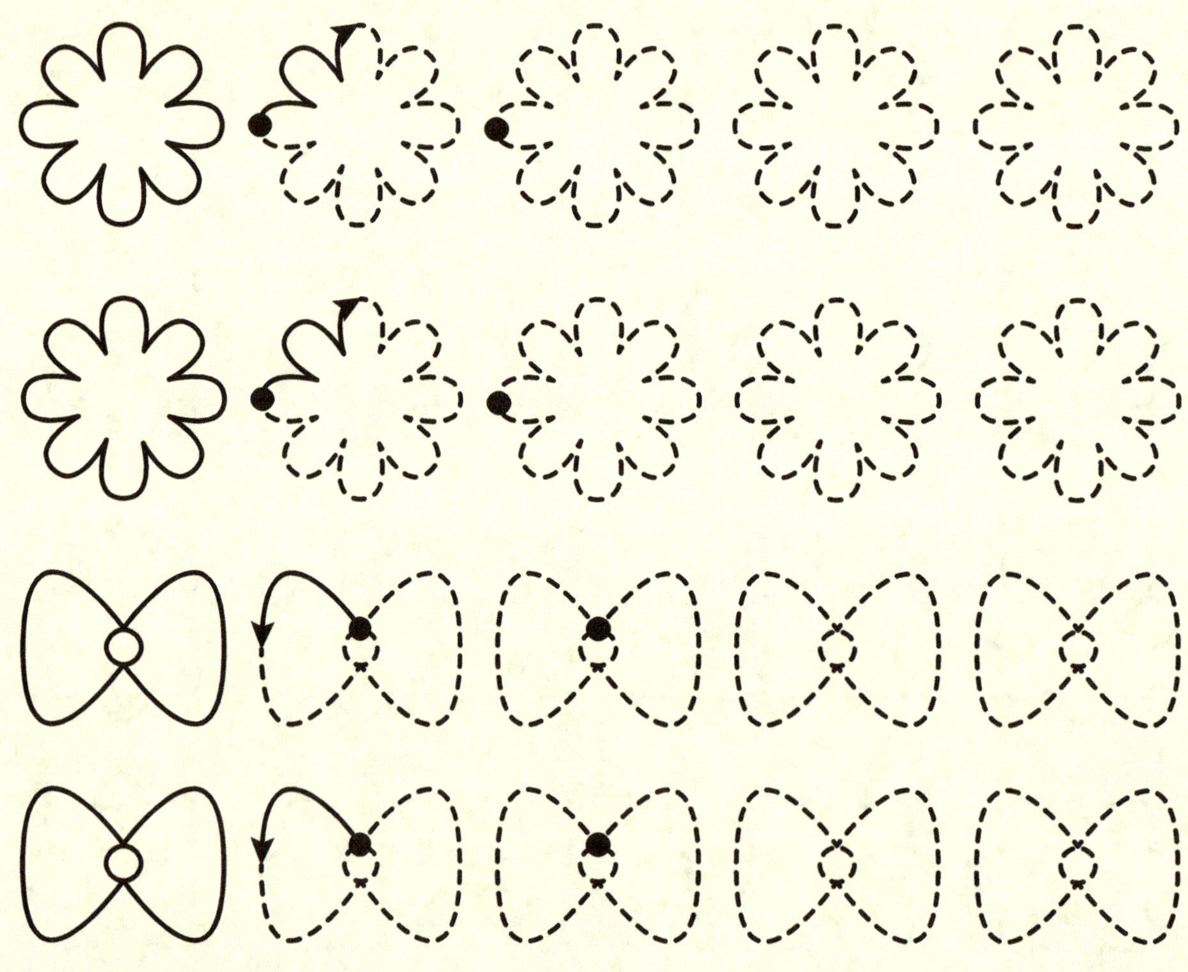

TRACING SHAPES

Trace the lines in each row.

now, let's try some line tracing activities!! it's fun! good luck!

I CAN TRACE LINES

Trace the lines in each row then write your own.

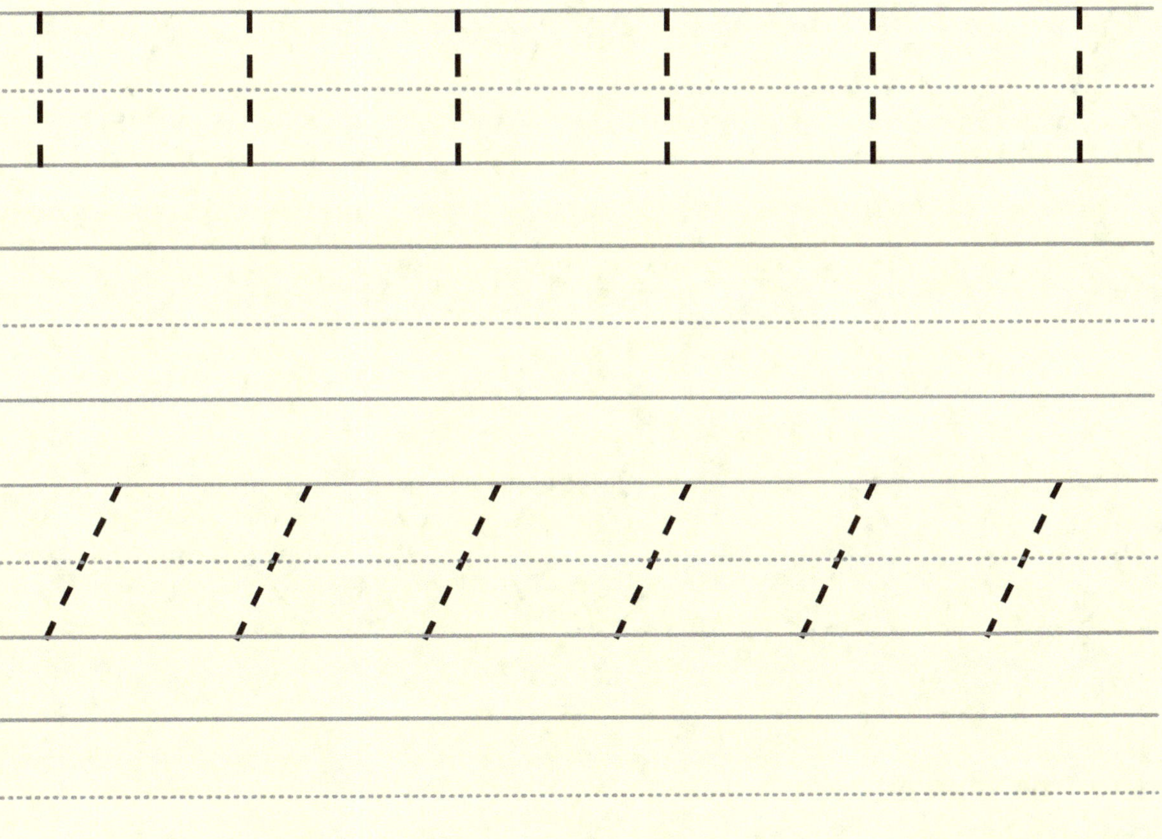

I CAN TRACE LINES

Trace the lines in each row then write your own.

I CAN TRACE LINES

Trace the lines in each row then write your own.

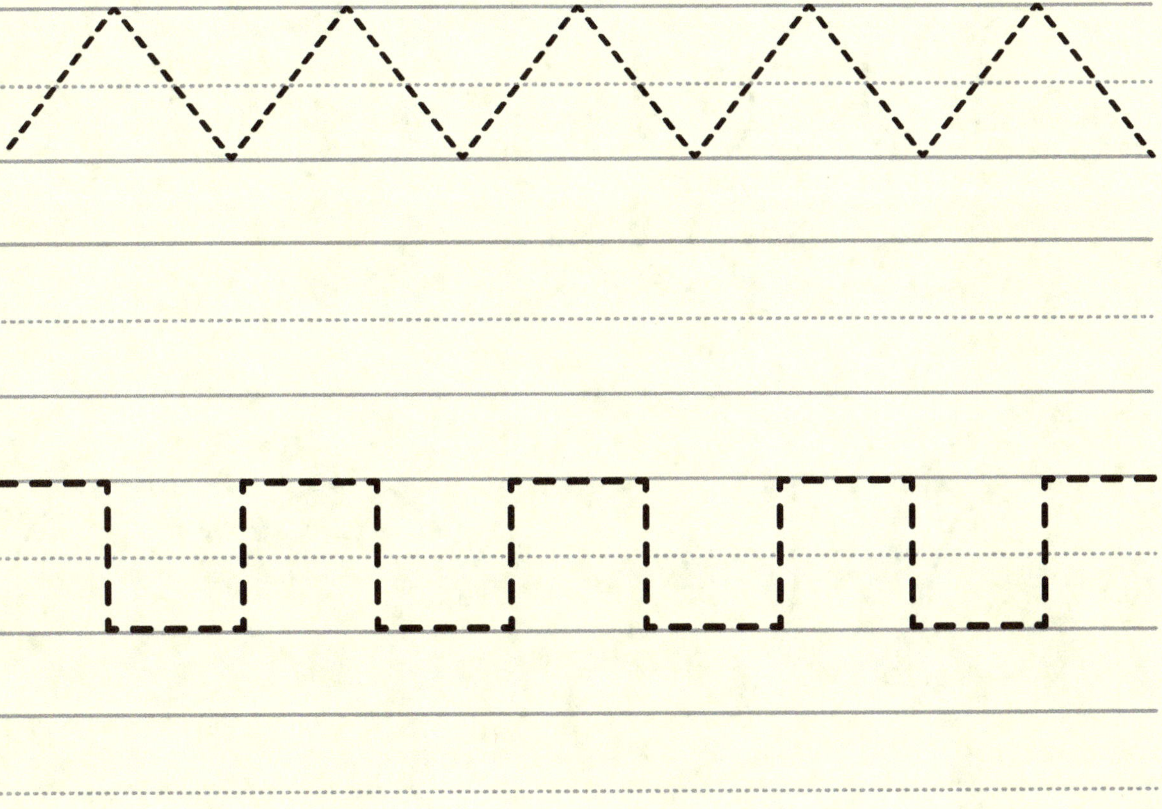

I CAN TRACE LINES

Trace the lines in each row then write your own.

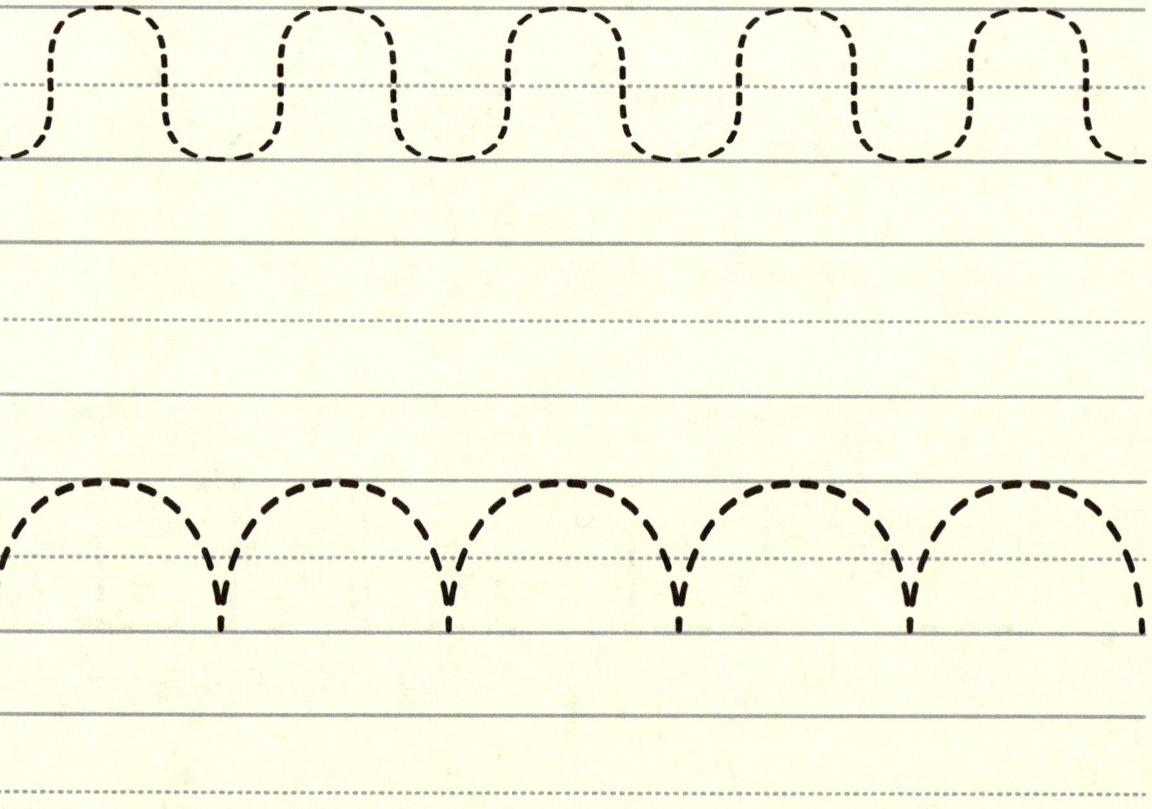

I CAN TRACE LINES

I CAN TRACE LINES

I CAN TRACE LINES

I CAN TRACE LINES

I CAN TRACE LINES

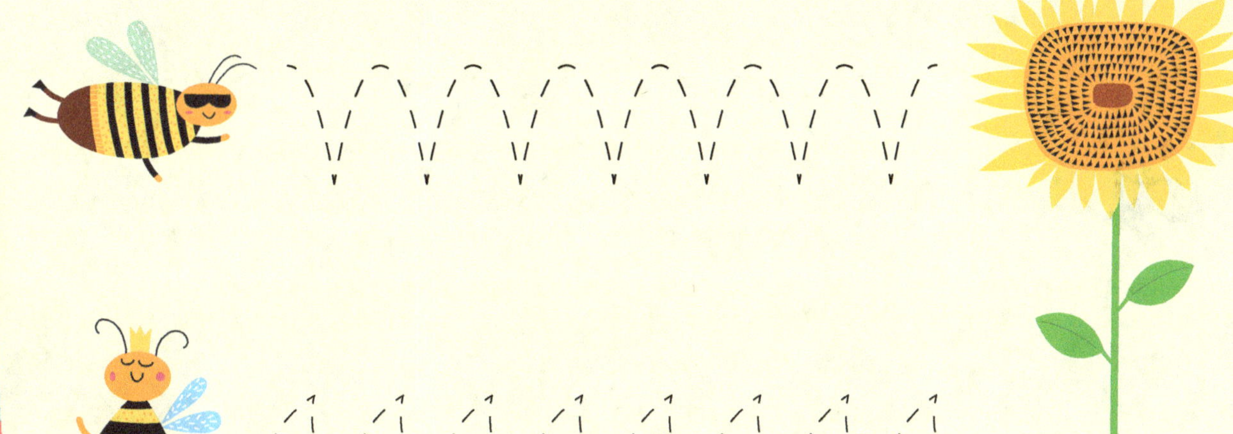

I CAN TRACE LINES

I CAN TRACE LINES

Trace the line from each animal to their food.

I CAN TRACE LINES

Trace the line from each animal to their food.

next is tracing
shapes
activities!
enjoy!

I CAN TRACE SHAPES

Trace the shape **CIRCLE** then color them.

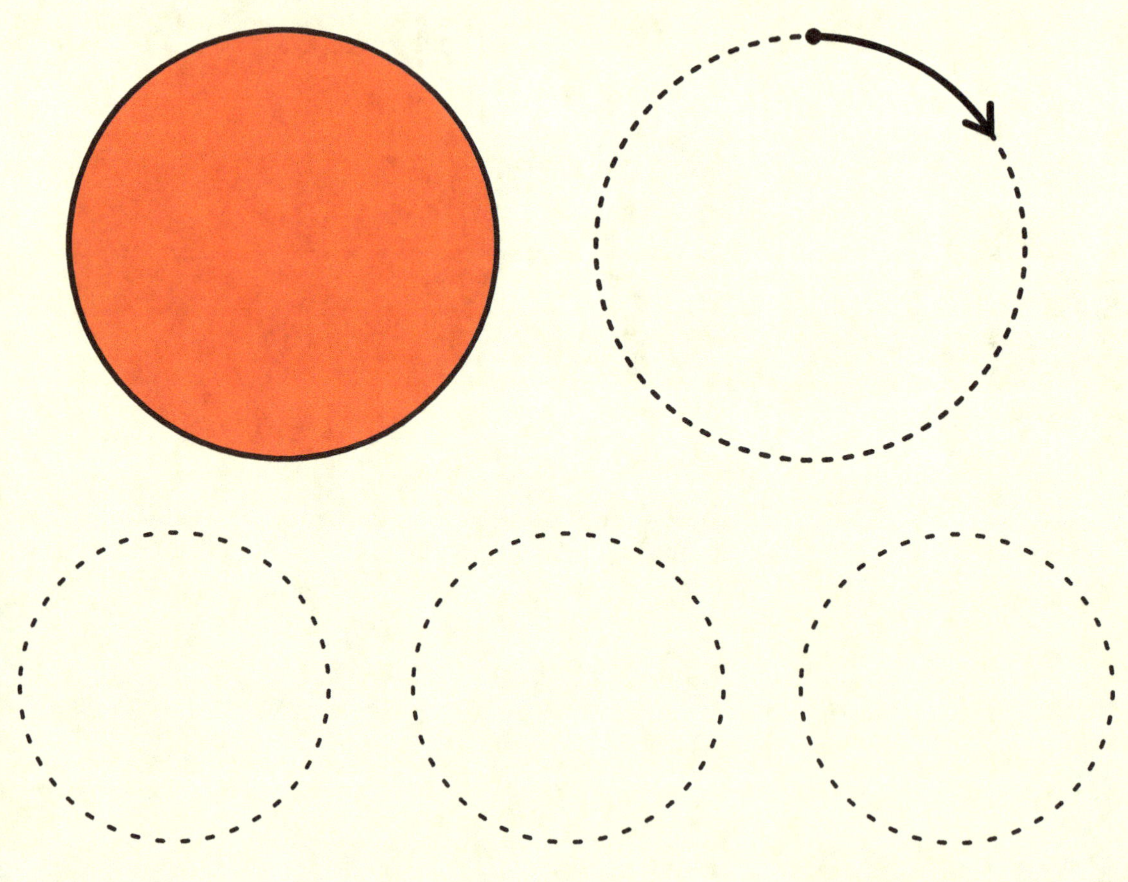

I CAN TRACE SHAPES

Trace the shape **ELLIPSE** then color them.

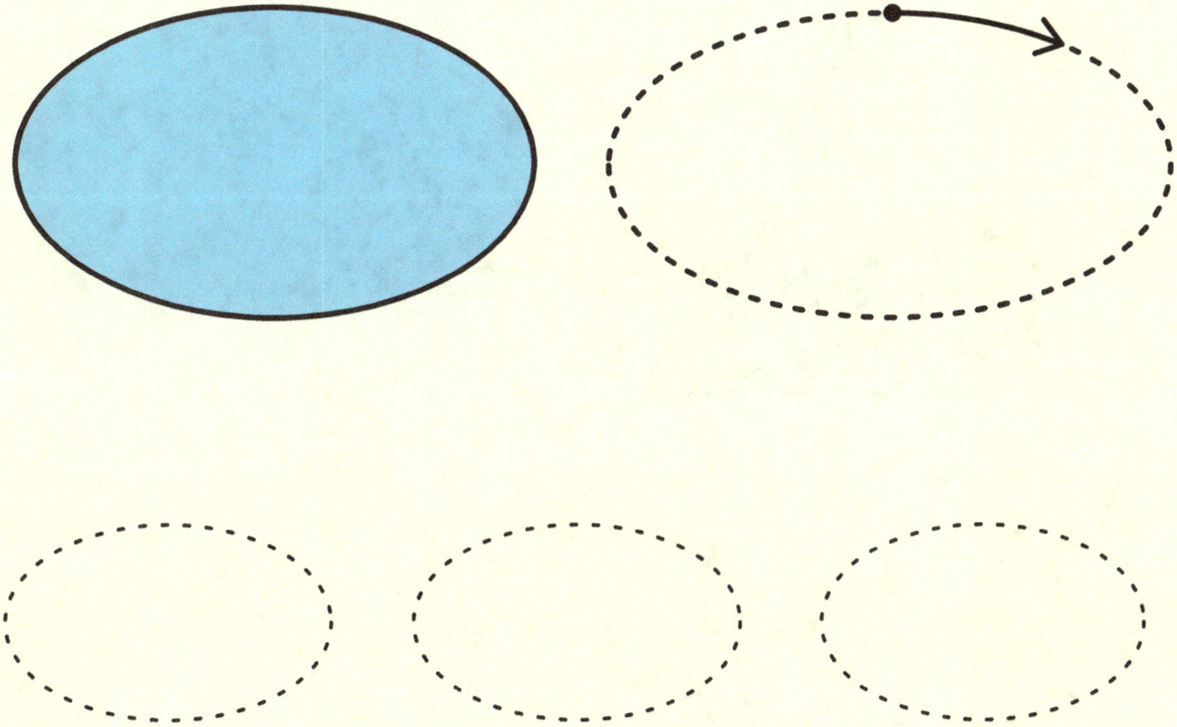

I CAN TRACE SHAPES

Trace the shape **TRIANGLE** then color them.

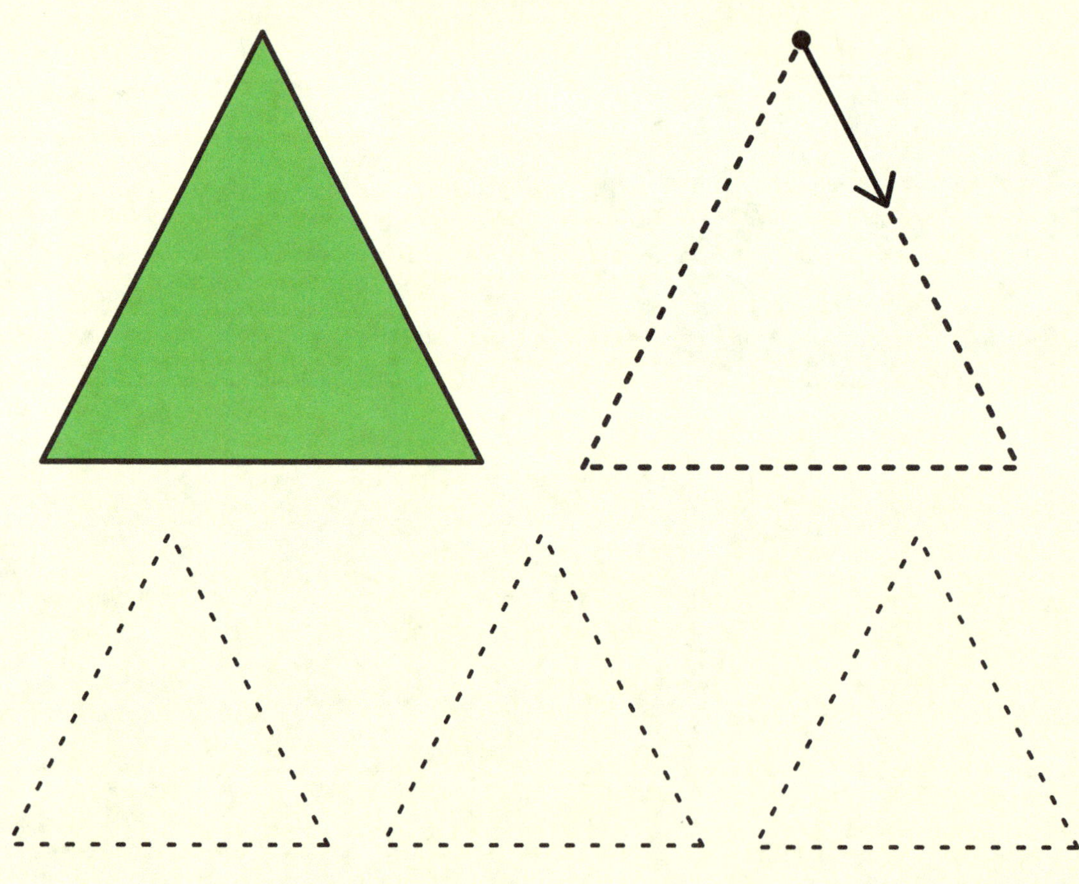

I CAN TRACE SHAPES

Trace the shape **SQUARE** then color them.

I CAN TRACE SHAPES

Trace the shape **RECTANGLE** then color them.

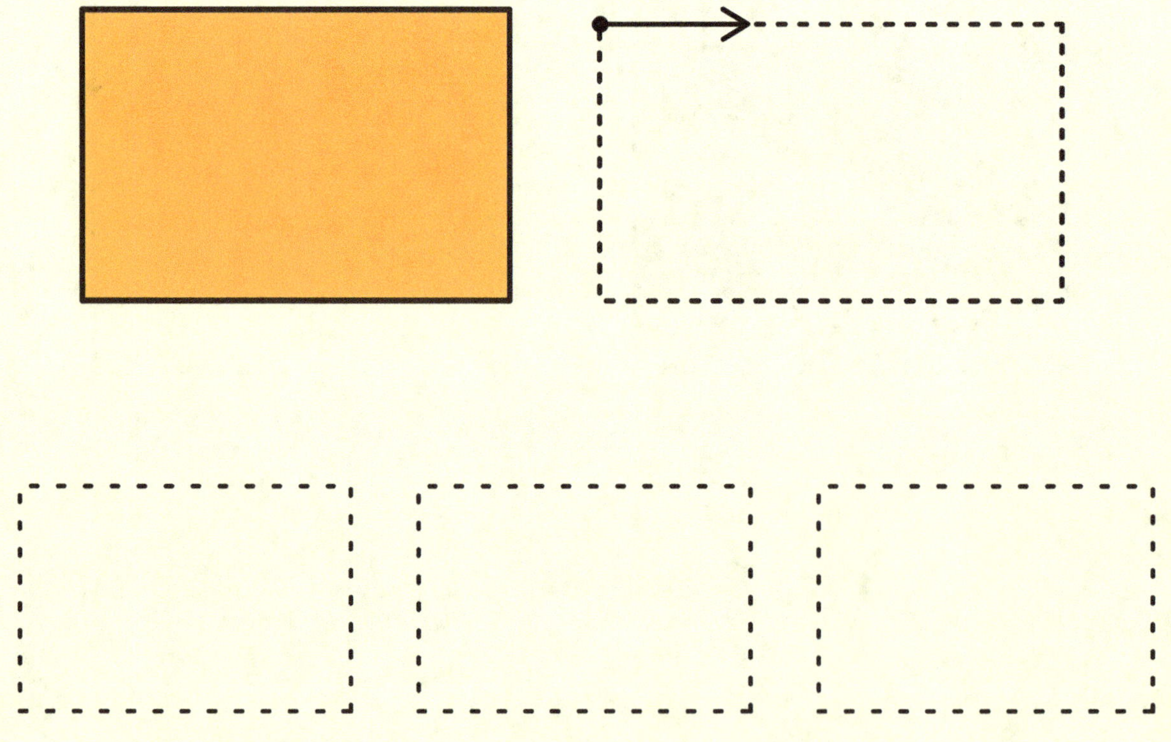

I CAN TRACE SHAPES

Trace the shape **TRAPEZIUM** then color them.

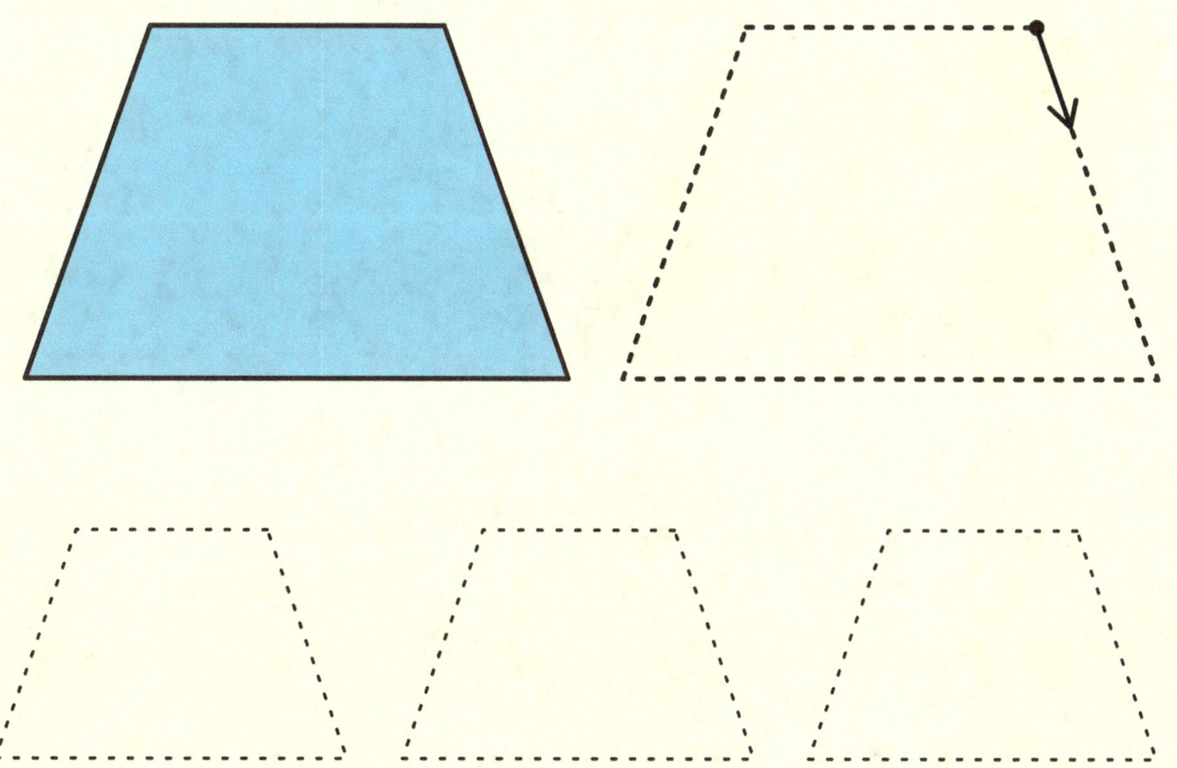

I CAN TRACE SHAPES

Trace the shape **PARALLELOGRAM** then color them.

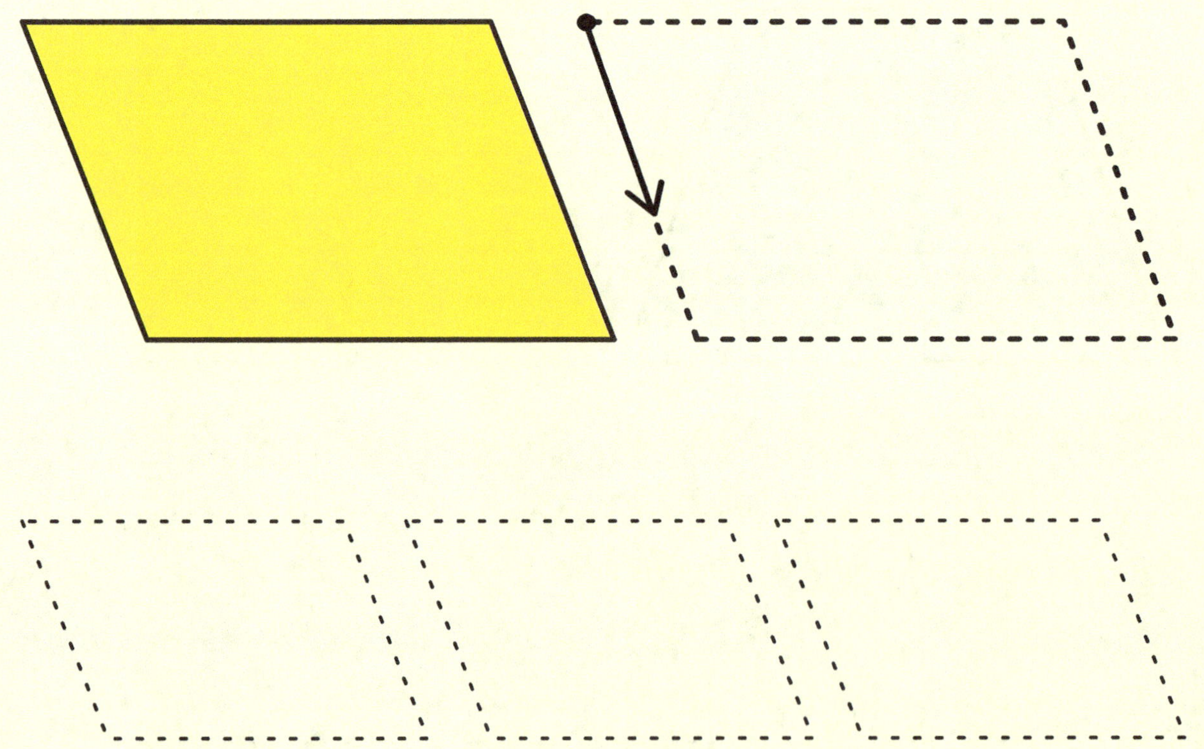

I CAN TRACE SHAPES

Trace the shape **PENTAGON** then color them.

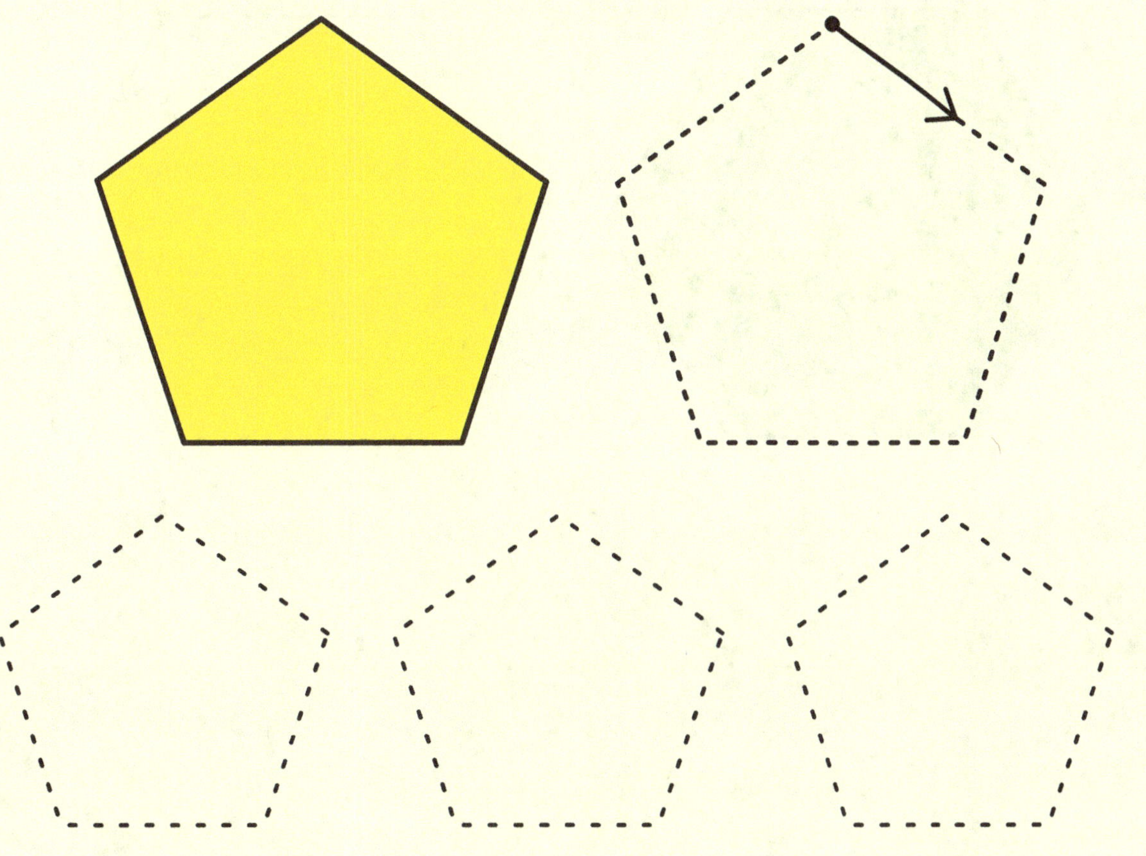

I CAN TRACE SHAPES

Trace the shape **HEXAGON** then color them.

I CAN TRACE SHAPES

Trace the shape **RHOMBUS** then color them.

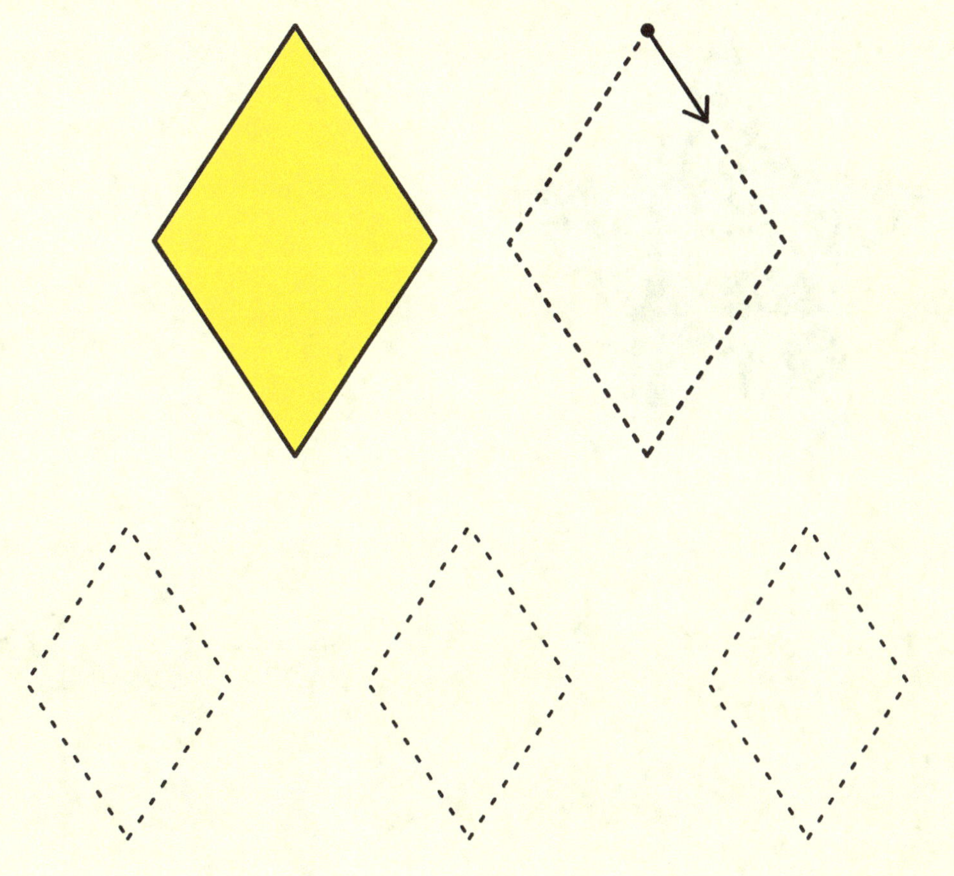

I CAN TRACE SHAPES

Trace the shape **STAR** then color them.

I CAN TRACE SHAPES

Trace the shape **QUATREFOIL** then color them.

I CAN TRACE SHAPES

Trace the shape **HEART** then color them.

I CAN TRACE SHAPES

Trace the shape **CROSS** then color them.

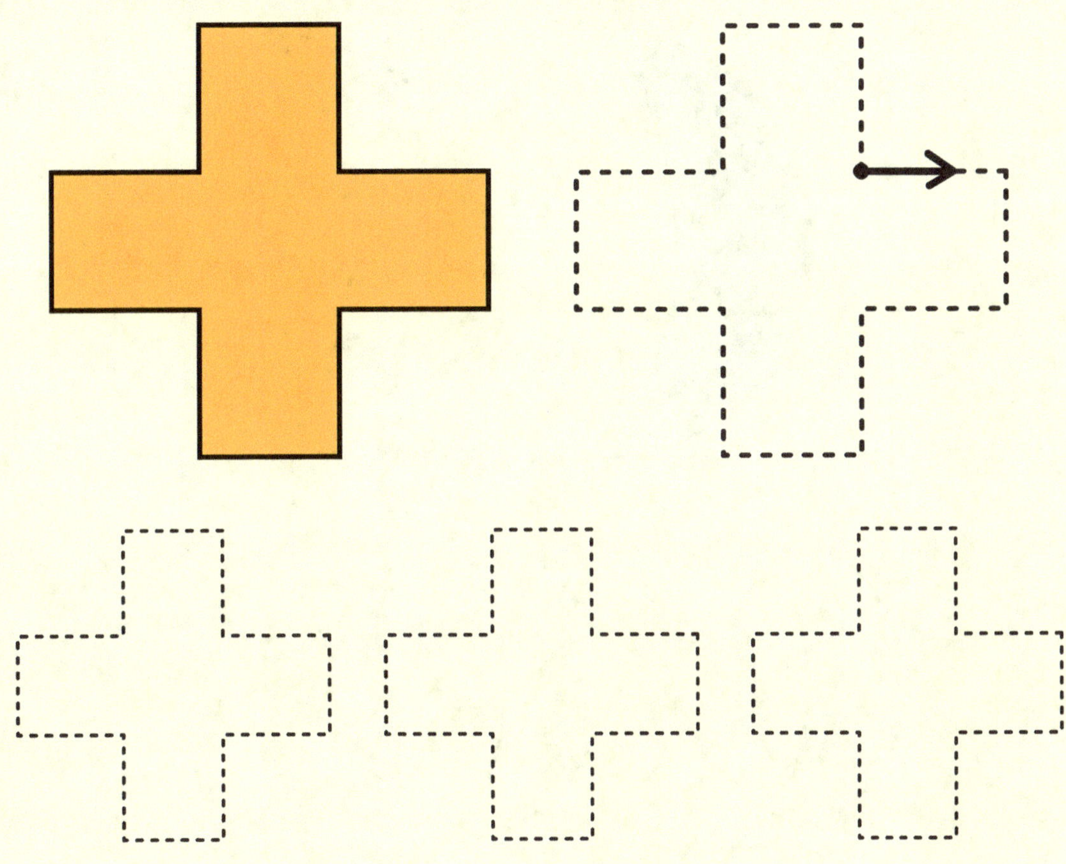

I CAN TRACE SHAPES

Trace the shape **CRESCENT** then color them.

I CAN TRACE SHAPES

Trace the shape **CURVILINEAR TRIANGLE** then color them.

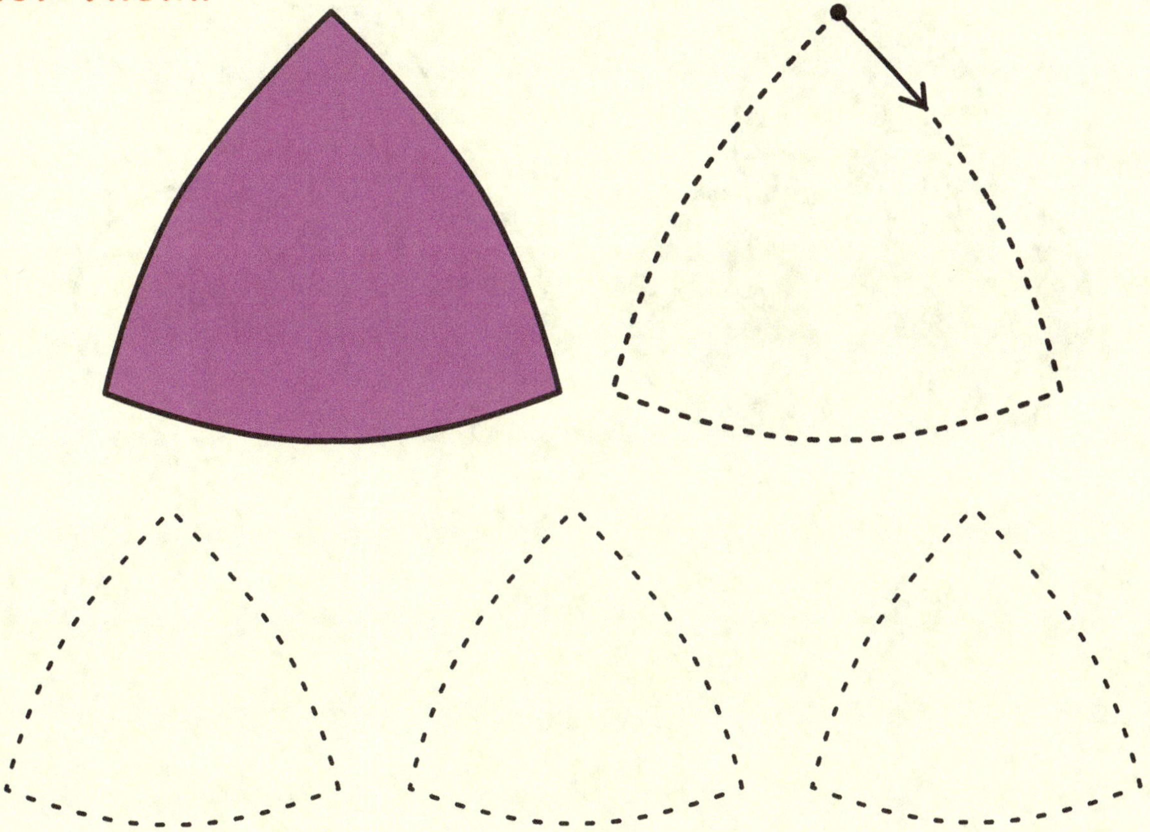

I CAN TRACE SHAPES

Trace the shape **TRIFOIL** then color them.

I CAN TRACE SHAPES

Trace the shape **EGG SHAPE** then color them.

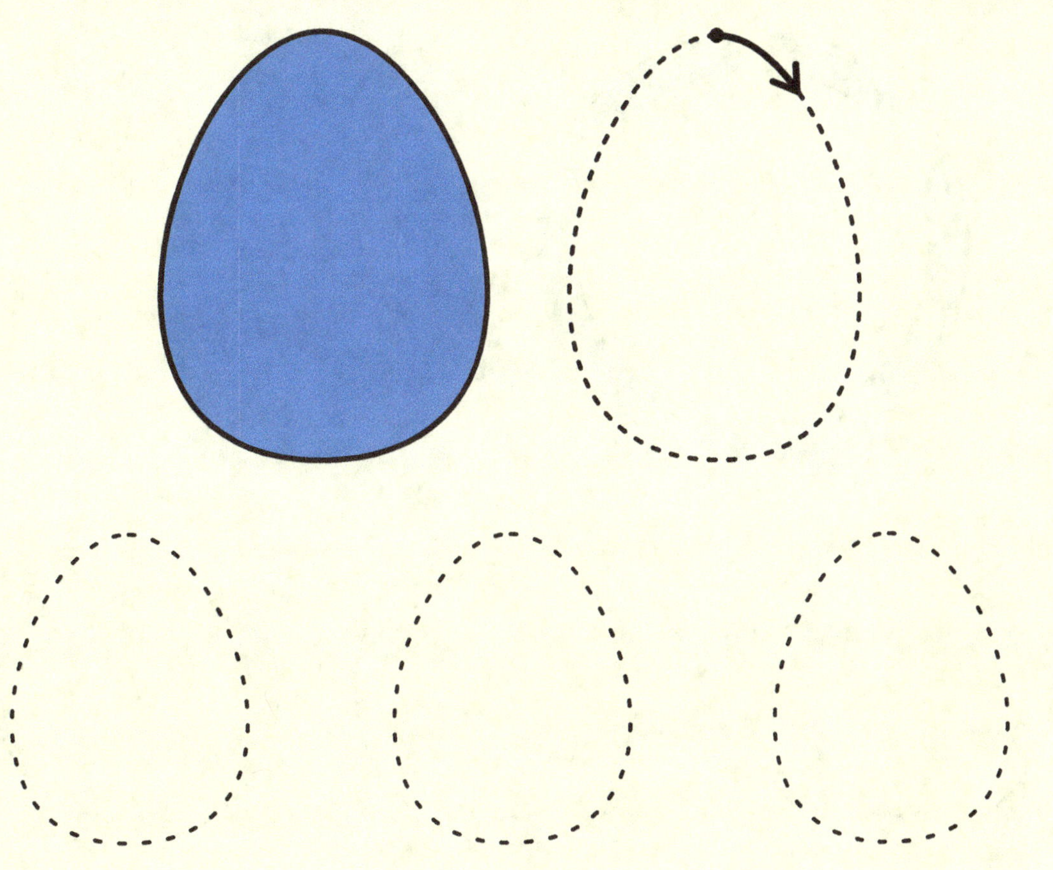

I CAN TRACE SHAPES

Trace the shape **RING** then color them.

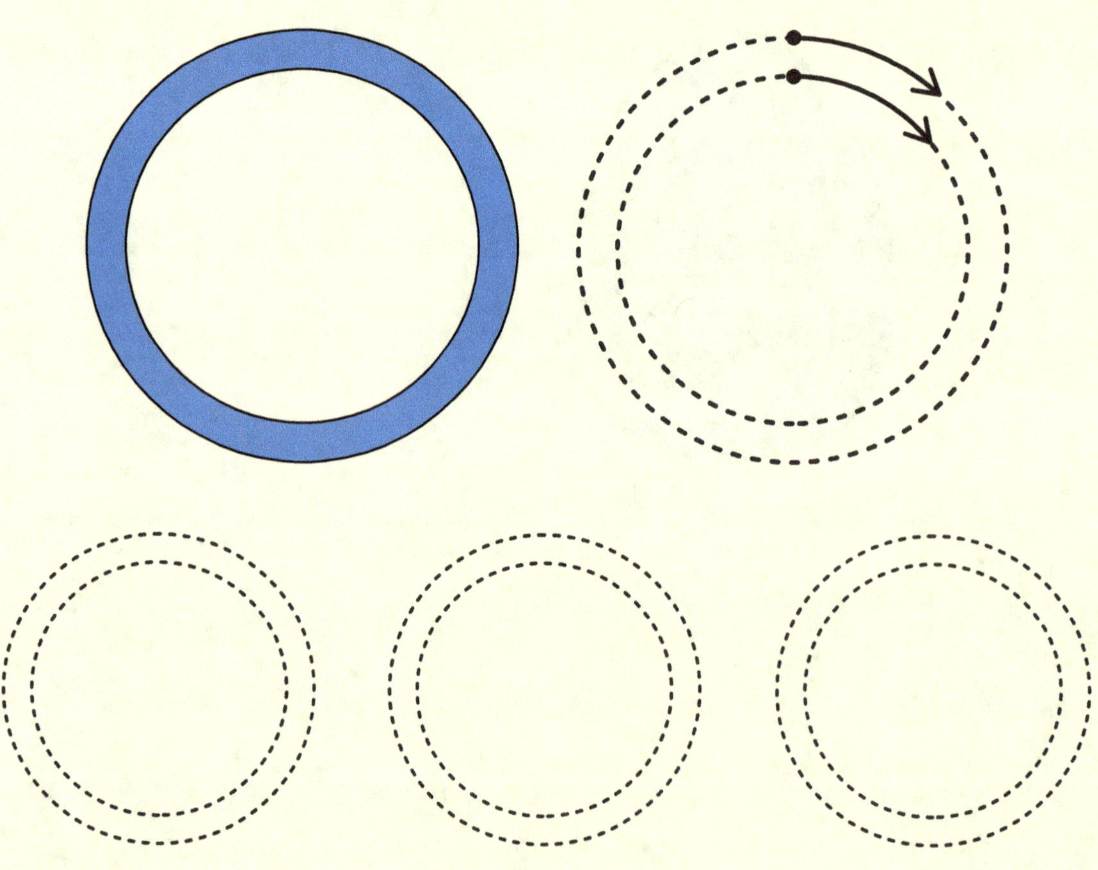

I CAN TRACE SHAPES

Trace the shape **ARROW** then color them.

I CAN DRAW

Trace the dashed lines of the images then color them.

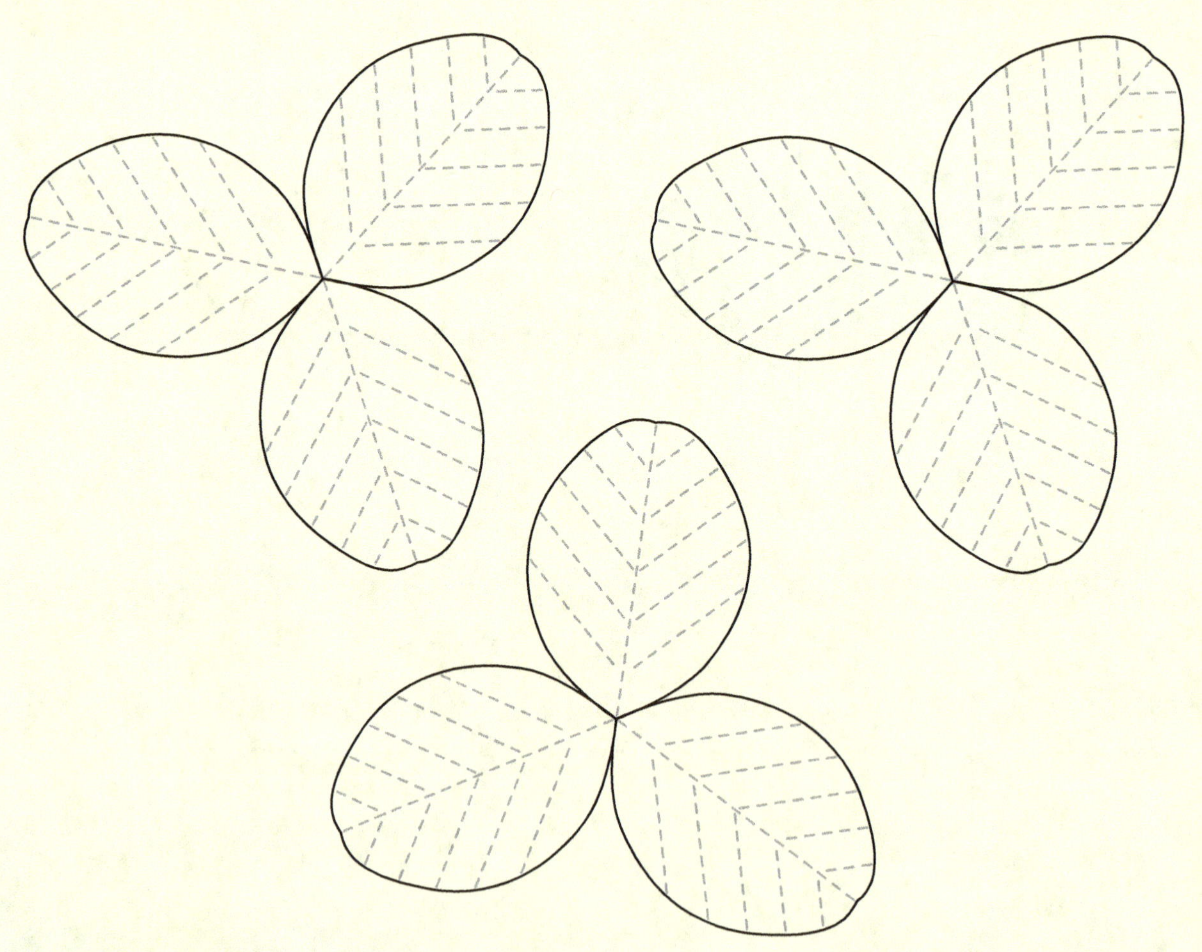

I CAN DRAW

Trace the dashed lines of the images then color them.

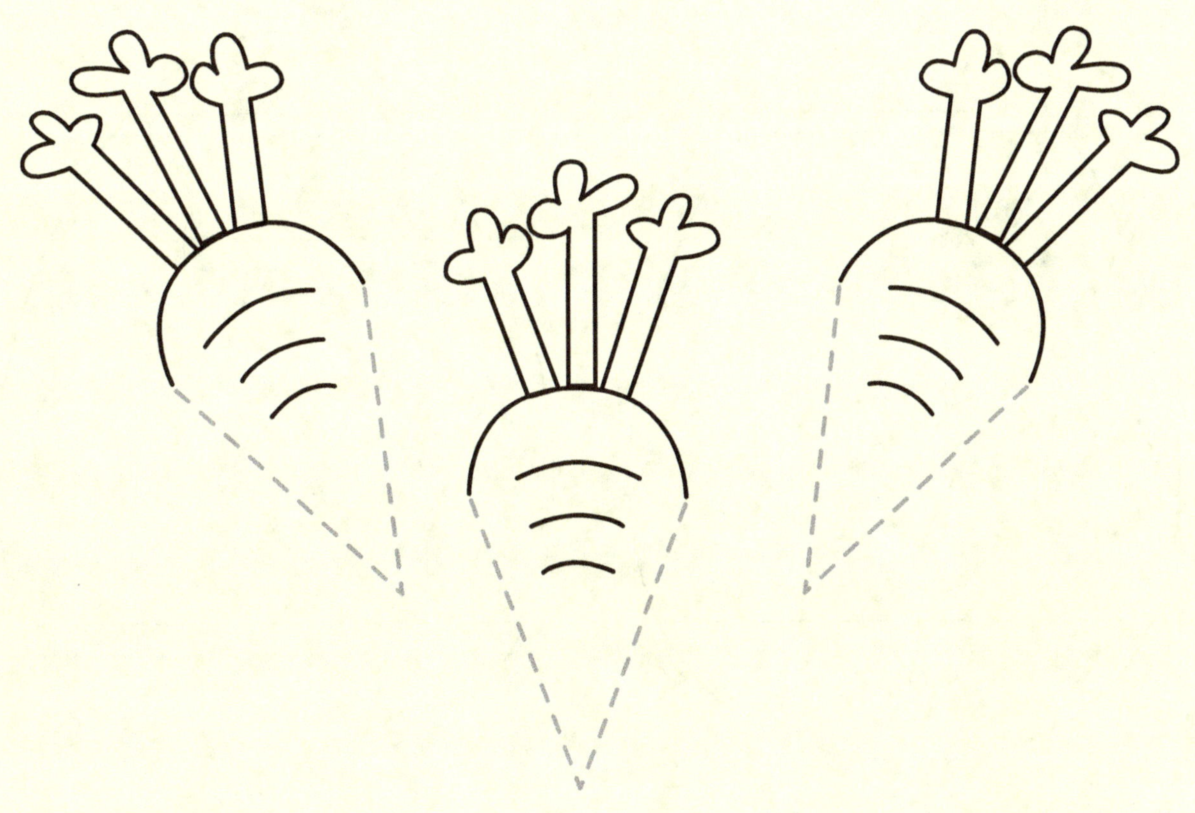

I CAN DRAW

Trace the dashed lines of the images then color them.

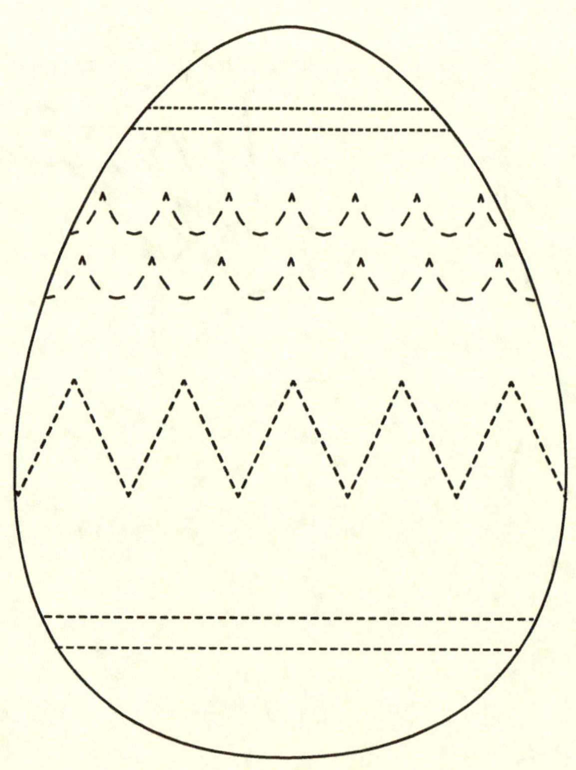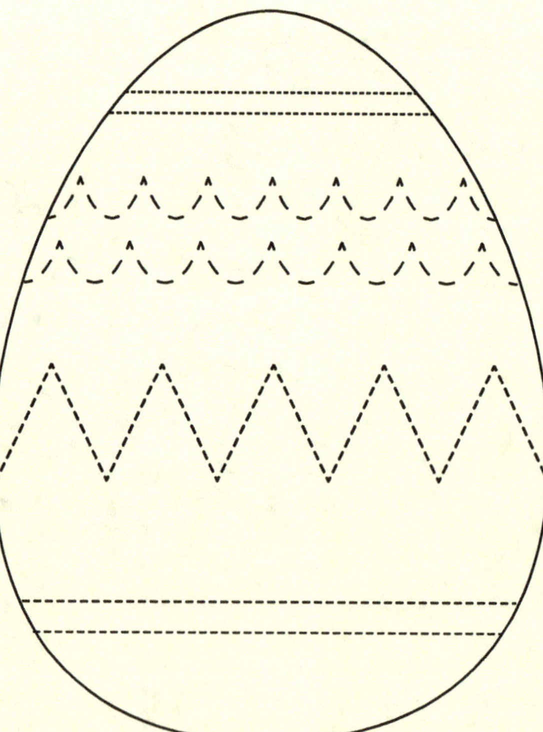

I CAN DRAW

Trace the dashed lines of the images then color them.

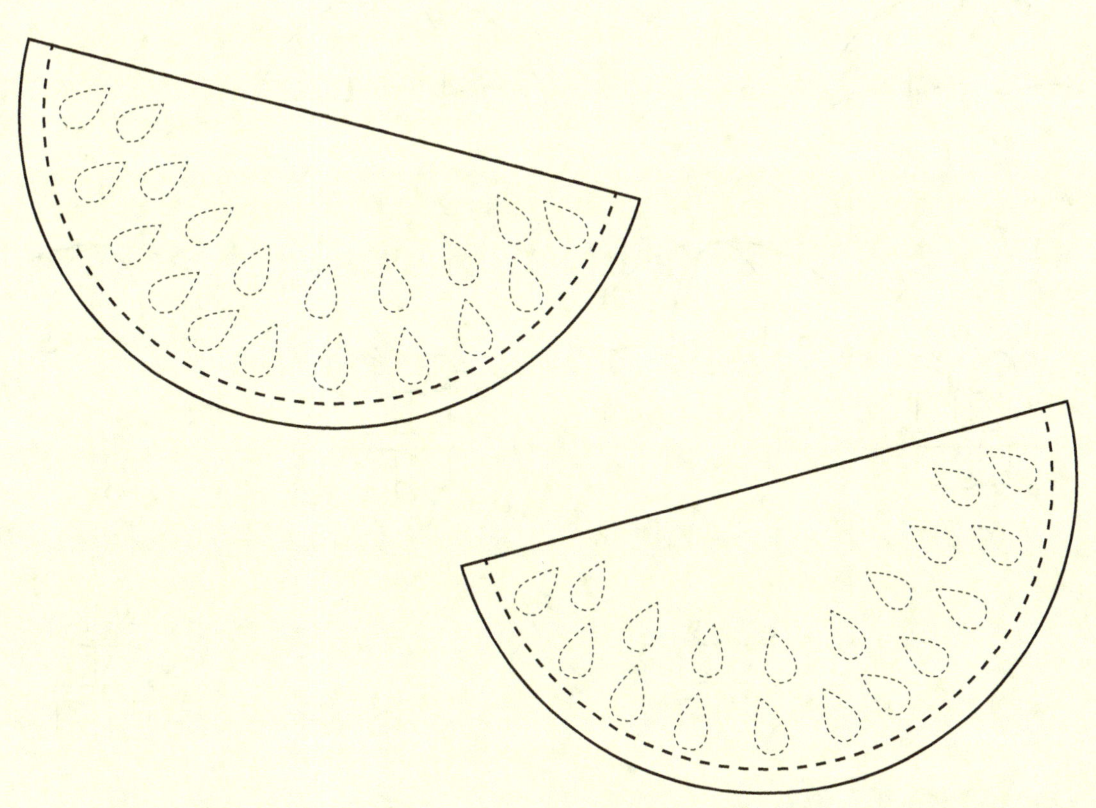

I CAN DRAW

Trace the dashed lines of the images then color them.

I CAN DRAW

Trace the dashed lines of the images then color them.

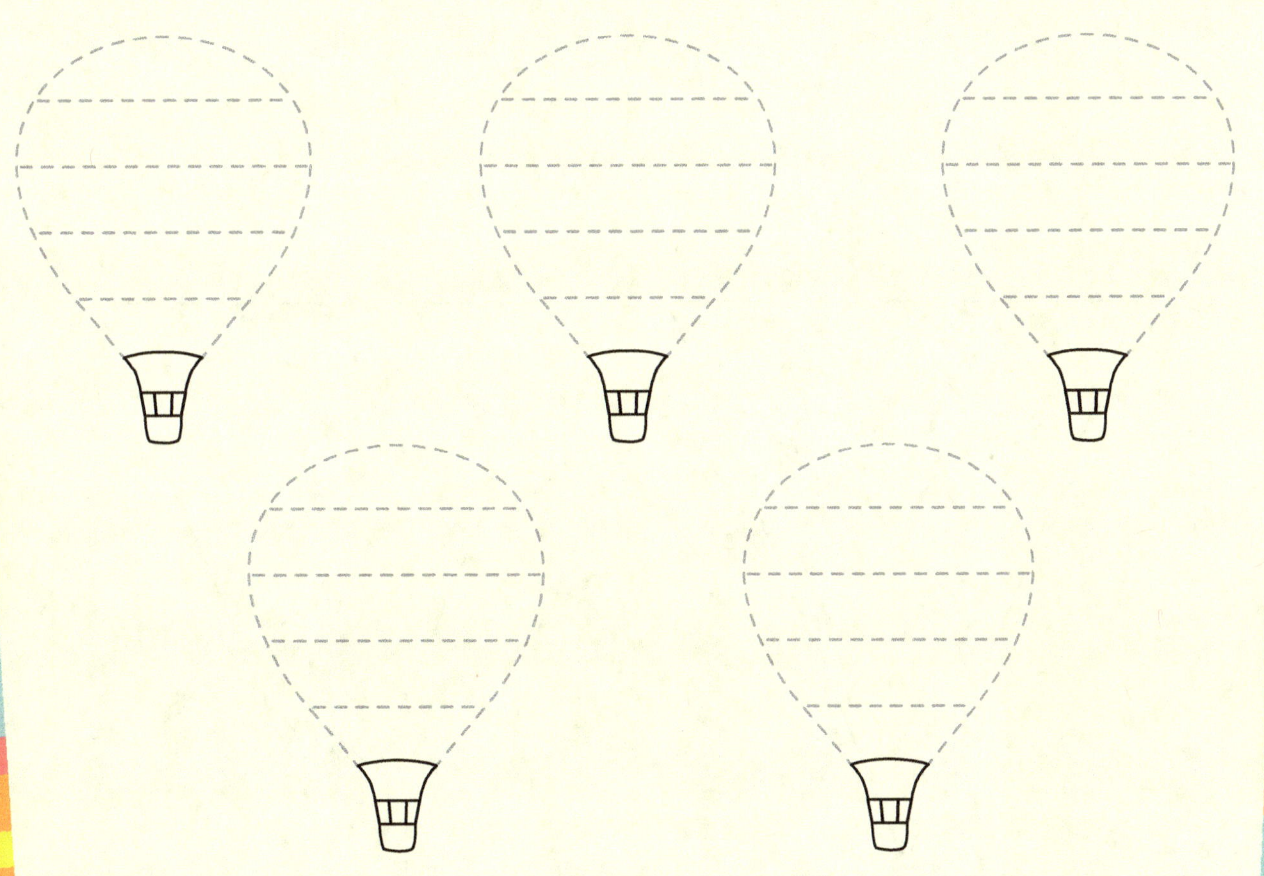

I CAN DRAW

Trace the dashed lines of the images then color them.

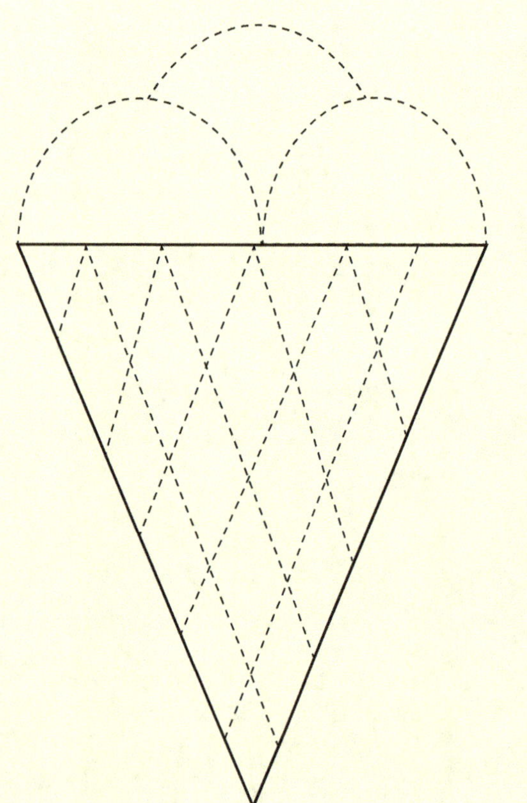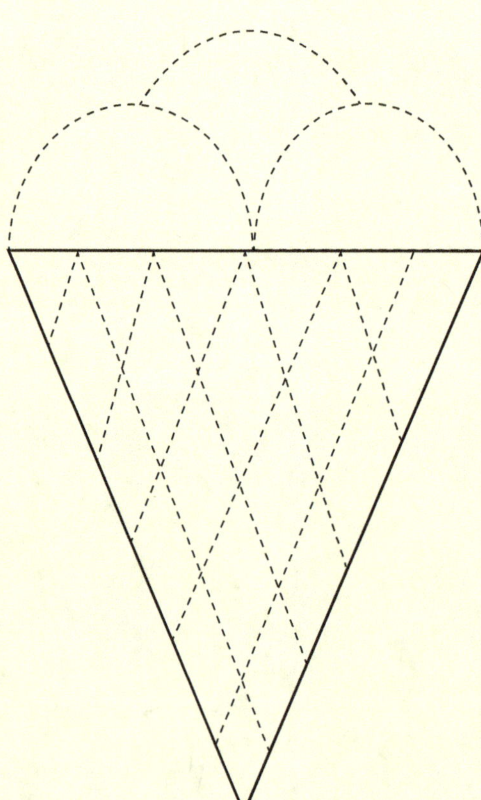

I CAN DRAW

Trace the dashed lines of the images then color them.

Visit
BABY PROFESSOR
EDUCATION KIDS
www.BabyProfessorBooks.com
to download Free Baby Professor eBooks
and view our catalog of new and exciting
Children's Books